NEW YORK
3rd Grade ELA
Test Prep

FOR

Common Core
Learning
Standards

teachers' treasures, inc.

Plano, TX

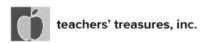

INTRODUCTION

This resource is not intended to be another worksheet to be given to students as a Common Core Learning Standards review. It is the intent of the authors that the questions be used to assess and manage students' understanding of the concepts assessed on Common Core State Standards Initiative.

This book is focused on the Common Core Standards for Reading Literature and Reading Informational Text. There are several questions for each Common Core Standard Reading Literature and Informational Text standard. We recommend you create a page made up of questions from three Common Core Standards. The answers can serve as a diagnostic tool to determine WHY the student had an incorrect answer. The answer to the student's misunderstanding is NOT another worksheet, but a re-teaching of the skill, using different instructional strategies.

The reason for incorrect answers is often the result of the student using an incorrect procedure. Most of the errors we see as teachers are the same each year. Students apply a rule in an inappropriate way. Many times they will even say to us, "That's what you said to do." They see logic in the way they have applied the rule even though it is incorrect. Therefore, it is imperative to determine WHY a student chose an incorrect answer to a question. The best way to determine this is to ask the student to explain their reasoning to you.

All questions in this product are aligned to the current Common Core State Standards Initiative.

3rd Grade
English Language Arts Test Prep

FOR

Common Core
Standards

Table of Contents

GRADE 3 ENGLISH LANGUAGE ARTS
COMMON CORE STATE STANDARDS INITIATIVE

Reading Literature - Key Ideas and Details	RL.3.1

Ask and answer questions to demonstrate understanding of a text, referring explicitly to the text as the basis for the answers.

Reading Literature – Key Ideas and Details	RL.3.2

Recount stories, including fables, folktales, and myths from diverse cultures; determine the central message, lesson, or moral and explain how it is conveyed through key details in the text.

Reading Literature – Key Ideas and Details	RL.3.3

Describe characters in a story (e.g., their traits, motivations, or feelings) and explain how their actions contribute to the sequence of events.

Reading Literature – Craft and Structure	RL.3.4

Determine the meaning of words and phrases as they are used in a text, distinguishing literal from nonliteral language.

Reading Literature – Craft and Structure	RL.3.5

Refer to parts of stories, dramas, and poems when writing or speaking about a text, using terms such as chapter, scene, and stanza; describe how each successive part builds on earlier sections.

Reading Literature – Craft and Structure	RL.3.6

Distinguish their own point of view from that of the narrator or those of the characters.

Reading Literature – Integration of Knowledge and Ideas	RL.3.7

Explain how specific aspects of a text's illustrations contribute to what is conveyed by the words in a story (e.g., create mood, emphasize aspects of a character or setting).

Reading Literature – Integration of Knowledge and Ideas	RL.3.8

(RL.3.8 not applicable to literature)

Reading Literature – Integration of Knowledge and Ideas	RL.3.9

Compare and contrast the themes, settings, and plots of stories written by the same author about the same or similar characters (e.g., in books from a series).

Reading Literature – Integration of Knowledge and Ideas	RL.3.10

By the end of the year, read and comprehend literature, including stories, dramas, and poetry, at the high end of the grades 2–3 text complexity band independently and proficiently.

Reading Informational Text – Key Ideas and Details | **RI.3.1**

Ask and answer questions to demonstrate understanding of a text, referring explicitly to the text as the basis for the answers.

Reading Informational Text – Key Ideas and Details | **RI.3.2**

Determine the main idea of a text; recount the key details and explain how they support the main idea.

Reading Informational Text – Key Ideas and Details | **RI.3.3**

Describe the relationship between a series of historical events, scientific ideas or concepts, or steps in technical procedures in a text, using language that pertains to time, sequence, and cause/effect.

Reading Informational Text – Craft and Structure | **RI.3.4**

Determine the meaning of general academic and domain-specific words and phrases in a text relevant to a *grade 3 topic or subject area.*

Reading Informational Text – Craft and Structure | **RI.3.5**

Use text features and search tools (e.g., key words, sidebars, hyperlinks) to locate information relevant to a given topic efficiently.

Reading Informational Text – Craft and Structure | **RI.3.6**

Distinguish their own point of view from that of the author of a text.

Reading Informational Text – Integration of Knowledge and Ideas | **RI.3.7**

Use information gained from illustrations (e.g., maps, photographs) and the words in a text to demonstrate understanding of the text (e.g., where, when, why, and how key events occur).

Reading Informational Text – Integration of Knowledge and Ideas | **RI.3.8**

Describe the logical connection between particular sentences and paragraphs in a text (e.g., comparison, cause/effect, first/second/third in a sequence).

Reading Informational Text – Integration of Knowledge and Ideas | **RI.3.9**

Compare and contrast the most important points and key details presented in two texts on the same topic.

Reading Informational Text – Range of Reading and Level of Text Complexity | **RI.3.10**

By the end of the year, read and comprehend informational texts, including history/social studies, science, and technical texts, at the high end of the grades 2–3 text complexity band independently and proficiently.

Luis Must Make a Choice

Luis went to the city library to find some books to take on his vacation. He likes to read each night before he goes to sleep, and he also likes to read in the car if he gets bored. Just as Luis was heading to the checkout counter with three books he had selected, he noticed a shelf of special books labeled, "FAVORITES." Luis knew he was only allowed to check out one book from this shelf during each library visit. Because he saw two books on the shelf that looked <u>fascinating</u>, he knew he would have to make a decision on which book to check out. He read these summaries on the books' covers to help him make his choice.

STORIES FROM THE SEA

If you enjoy mysteries, then you must read this <u>collection</u> of stories about the <u>adventures</u> some people had while sailing on many different seas. The stories <u>vary</u> from those of dangerous pirates to stories of <u>weird</u> weather happenings.

In addition to stories, there are many pictures. You'll find out why these people were on the ships or boats, their <u>destinations</u>, and what happened to them.

These stories are not for the weak of heart. Unless you like to feel frightened, you should choose another book. The author does not want anyone to die of fright while reading this book.

NATIVE AMERICAN CHIEFS AND LEADERS

This is your chance to learn about many of the great Indian chiefs and leaders you have read about or seen on TV and in the movies.

This book tells interesting <u>personal</u> facts about these <u>courageous</u> men. For example, Chief Sitting Bull, leader of the Sioux, fought in the battle of Little Big Horn, where General George Custer and his men died.

You will find out about the families of these great chiefs and leaders, <u>the</u> customs of their tribes, and where many of their <u>descendants</u> live today. And there's more — you will see real photos of these great men and maps of how our country looked long ago.

Included:
* Chief Sitting Bull, Sioux
* Quanah Parker, Comanche
* Chief Joseph, Nez Perce
* Tecumseh, Shawnee
* Bacon Rind, Osage
* Geronimo, Apache
* Sequoya, Cherokee
* Dull Knife, Cheyenne

Name _____   Date_____

Common Core Standard RI.3.4, Common Core Standard RL.3.4

☐ **In this story, the word <u>collection</u> means --**

◯ one

◯ a set of more than one

◯ book

◯ from the sea

Common Core Standard RI.3.4

☐ **In this story, the word <u>destinations</u> means --**

◯ the beginning of a journey

◯ the middle of a journey

◯ the end of a journey

◯ experiences

Common Core Standard RI.3.4

☐ **In this story, the word <u>personal</u> means --**

◯ private

◯ informed

◯ well known

◯ interesting

Common Core Standard RI.3.4

☐ In this story, the word <u>fascinating</u> means --

- ◯ good
- ◯ interesting
- ◯ long
- ◯ boring

Common Core Standard RI.3.4

☐ In this story, the word <u>vary</u> means --

- ◯ same
- ◯ unusual
- ◯ long
- ◯ change

Common Core Standard RI.3.4

☐ In this story, the word <u>descendants</u> means --

- ◯ people related to each other
- ◯ group
- ◯ people following the tribe's leader
- ◯ houses

Common Core Standard RI.3.4

☐ **In this story, the word <u>adventures</u> means --**

⬭ common experiences

⬭ secrets

⬭ groups of people going on a trip

⬭ unusual and exciting events

Common Core Standard RI.3.4

☐ **In this story, the word <u>weird</u> means --**

⬭ normal

⬭ hurricanes

⬭ odd

⬭ weather patterns

Common Core Standard RI.3.4

☐ **In this story, the word <u>courageous</u> means --**

⬭ sorry

⬭ fearless

⬭ weak

⬭ dead

Common Core Standard RI.3.3

☐ **Why did Luis go to the library?**

◯ To see his friends

◯ To get books to take with him on his vacation

◯ To find out about Chief Sitting Bull

◯ To learn about ocean storms

Common Core Standard RI.3.3

☐ **If Luis had not seen the shelf of special books, how many books would he have checked out?**

◯ Three

◯ Four

◯ Two

◯ Five

Common Core Standard RI.3.3

☐ **When does Luis usually read in the car?**

◯ On vacations

◯ Going to school

◯ On the bus

◯ When he gets bored

Common Core Standard RI.3.8

☐ **Which of these will Luis do last?**

○ Look at the books in the library

○ Look at the books on the special shelf

○ Read the books' covers

○ Check out the books he chooses

Common Core Standard RI.3.8

☐ **What happened after Luis saw the shelf of "FAVORITES?"**

○ He went to the library.

○ He read the summaries of two books.

○ He found three books to check out.

○ He chose one of the special books.

Common Core Standard RI.3.8

☐ **When did Luis read the summaries on the books' covers?**

○ After he left the library

○ Before he went to the library

○ Before he chose a book from the "FAVORITES" shelf

○ During his vacation

Common Core Standard RI.3.7

☐ **Where did most of the story take place?**

○ At school

○ On vacation

○ In the library

○ At Luis's house

Common Core Standard RI.3.7

☐ **Where will Luis take the library books?**

○ On his vacation

○ To his classroom

○ To his grandparents

○ To the library

Common Core Standard RI.3.7

☐ **Where would you find the book <u>Native American Chiefs and Leaders</u>?**

○ In Luis's room

○ On the "FAVORITES" shelf

○ In the school library

○ In Luis's book bag

Common Core Standard RI.3.6

☐ **What kind of reader would probably want to read** <u>Stories from the Sea</u>**?**

    ◯   Someone who likes mystery stories

    ◯   Someone who owns a sailboat

    ◯   Someone who knows a pirate

    ◯   Someone who collects stories

Common Core Standard RI.3.6

☐ **Will a reader find information about Chief Henry Standing Bear in the book** <u>Native American Chiefs and Leaders</u>**?**

    ◯   Maybe

    ◯   Probably

    ◯   No

    ◯   Yes

Common Core Standard RI.3.7

☐ **How many Indian chiefs and leaders will a reader learn about in** <u>Native American Chiefs and Leaders</u>**?**

    ◯   Seven

    ◯   One

    ◯   Nine

    ◯   Eight

Common Core Standard RI.3.2, Common Core Standard RL.3.2

☐ **Which sentence tells what this story is mostly about?**

- ◯ Luis went to the library and found a book on sailing.

- ◯ Luis went to the library where he selected books to take on his vacation.

- ◯ Luis likes to read mysteries about the sea.

- ◯ Luis is going on a vacation, and he likes to read stories about the sea and Indians.

Common Core Standard RI.3.2, Common Core Standard RL.3.2

☐ **What is the main idea of this story?**

- ◯ Luis found some interesting books at the library to take on his vacation.

- ◯ Luis wants to read about Indian chiefs while he is on vacation.

- ◯ Luis went to the library and found a book about pirates.

- ◯ Luis will check out three books.

Common Core Standard RI.3.2, Common Core Standard RL.3.2

☐ **Which of these describes what happens in this story?**

- ◯ The library has many interesting books including books about pirates and Indians.

- ◯ Luis likes to read.

- ◯ Luis is going on a vacation soon.

- ◯ When Luis visited the library, he found several good books to take on his vacation.

Common Core Standard RI.3.3, Common Core Standard RL.3.5, Common Core Standard RI.3.6

☐ **Luis's main problem was that --**

⬭ he was going on vacation

⬭ he had gone to the library

⬭ he could only select one book from the special shelf

⬭ he had checked out too many books

Common Core Standard RI.3.3, Common Core Standard RL.3.5, Common Core Standard RI.3.6

☐ **According to the story, what could create a problem for Luis?**

⬭ If he goes on vacation tomorrow

⬭ If he cannot decide which book to check out

⬭ If he stays at the library too long

⬭ If he reads <u>Native American Chiefs and Leaders</u>

Common Core Standard RI.3.3, Common Core Standard RL.3.5, Common Core Standard RI.3.6

☐ **According to the summary of <u>Stories from the Sea</u>, what could be a problem for the reader?**

⬭ The reader could be very frightened.

⬭ The reader could hurt her eyes.

⬭ The reader might not like mysteries.

⬭ The reader will read about pirates and storms.

Common Core Standard RI.3.6, Common Core Standard RL.3.6

☐ The library probably wants their readers to check out only one book from the "FAVORITES" shelf because --

◯ they are being selfish

◯ they want the books available for many readers

◯ there are only two books

◯ the books are very old

Common Core Standard RI.3.6, Common Core Standard RL.3.6

☐ In the future, Luis will most likely --

◯ not read any books from the library

◯ read the books from the school library

◯ check out five books

◯ check out other books from the "FAVORITES" shelf

Common Core Standard RI.3.6, Common Core Standard RL.3.6

☐ Why did Luis go to the library?

◯ To check out three books

◯ To find a book about pirates

◯ To get books to read on his vacation

◯ To learn about Indian chiefs

Common Core Standard RI.3.7

☐ **Many people would read <u>Native American Chiefs and Leaders</u> to –**

    ⬭ learn about the descendants of great Indian chiefs

    ⬭ learn how to be courageous

    ⬭ find more information on Indian foods

    ⬭ learn how to make war bonnets

Common Core Standard RI.3.7

☐ **All of the characters in <u>Native American Chiefs and Leaders</u> –**

    ⬭ lived in Texas

    ⬭ died in war

    ⬭ belonged to different tribes

    ⬭ are alive today

Common Core Standard RI.3.7

☐ **All of the stories in <u>Stories From The Sea</u> are about --**

    ⬭ pirates

    ⬭ storms

    ⬭ pictures

    ⬭ sailing adventures

Common Core Standard RI.3.8, Common Core Standard RI.3.6

☐ If a reader likes mysteries, he will probably enjoy <u>Stories from the Sea</u> because --

⬭ many of the sea adventures are not true

⬭ there are many stories about sea adventures

⬭ of the frightening suspense in these stories

⬭ he can learn

Common Core Standard RI.3.8, Common Core Standard RI.3.6

☐ If a reader likes history, she will like <u>Native American Chiefs and Leaders</u> because --

⬭ she will learn facts about important people of the past

⬭ she will learn about a hero

⬭ the book is short and easy to read

⬭ it is a new book

Common Core Standard RI.3.8, Common Core Standard RI.3.6

☐ If Luis chooses <u>Native American Chiefs and Leaders</u>, he will have maps and photos so he --

⬭ can travel

⬭ can see how and where the chiefs lived

⬭ can sympathize with the Indians

⬭ will not get bored

Common Core Standard RI.3.8

☐ **We know that Luis likes to read because –**

⬭ he went to the library

⬭ he is going on vacation

⬭ he read the books' summaries

⬭ he reads each night and sometimes in the car

Common Core Standard RI.3.8

☐ **Stories from the Sea is scary because**

⬭ it is about sea adventures

⬭ it is about mysterious adventures people had while sailing

⬭ it is a long book

⬭ the author does not want anyone to read it

Common Core Standard RL.3.3, Common Core Standard RI.3.8

☐ **We know that Chief Sitting Bull was a brave leader because**

⬭ he fought in the Little Big Horn battle

⬭ he lived long ago

⬭ he knew General George Custer

⬭ he belonged to the Sioux tribe

Common Core Standard RL.3.3, Common Core Standard RL.3.6

☐ How did Luis probably feel when he saw the two interesting books on the "FAVORITES" shelf?

⬭ Overwhelmed

⬭ Excited

⬭ Anxious

⬭ Nervous

Common Core Standard RL.3.3, Common Core Standard RL.3.6

☐ How would a reader probably feel about traveling by sea after reading Stories from the Sea?

⬭ Afraid

⬭ Excited

⬭ Informed

⬭ Tired

Common Core Standard RL.3.3, Common Core Standard RL.3.6

☐ How would a relative of Chief Joseph probably feel if he read Native American Chiefs and Leaders?

⬭ Silly

⬭ Lonely

⬭ Proud

⬭ Funny

Name _____   Date_____

Common Core Standard RI.3.6

☐ **Information in the summary of <u>Native American Chiefs and Leaders</u> suggests that --**

◯ this book contains many facts

◯ this book is not true

◯ these Indians were not famous

◯ the photos and maps are fakes

Common Core Standard RI.3.6

☐ **The reader can tell that <u>Stories From The Sea</u> --**

◯ is not true

◯ is funny

◯ is about mysterious happenings

◯ will make the reader want to go sailing

Common Core Standard RI.3.6

☐ **The author of <u>Native American Chiefs and Leaders</u> probably chose the characters featured in the book because --**

◯ he knew them

◯ they were very important

◯ they are dead

◯ they lived long ago

Common Core Standard RI.3.1, Common Core Standard RL.3.1

☐ **Which is a FACT in this story?**

⬭ Luis chose six books.

⬭ Luis will be afraid if he reads <u>Stories from the Sea</u>.

⬭ <u>Stories from the Sea</u> has pictures.

⬭ Luis will chose <u>Native American Chiefs and Leaders</u>.

Common Core Standard RI.3.1, Common Core Standard RL.3.1

☐ **Which of these is an OPINION in this story?**

⬭ Sea adventures are the most exciting to read about.

⬭ In <u>Native American Chiefs and Leaders</u> there is information about Chief Bacon Rind.

⬭ <u>Native American Chiefs and Leaders</u> has maps of our country.

⬭ <u>Stories from the Sea</u> has many different stories.

Common Core Standard RI.3.1, Common Core Standard RL.3.1

☐ **Which of these is a FACT in the story?**

⬭ Chief Sequoya is the most interesting Native American featured in the book.

⬭ Luis likes to be frightened, so he will read <u>Stories From The Sea</u>.

⬭ There are many descendants of the Indian chiefs alive today.

⬭ Luis went to the city library.

Fire Safety

Ms. Roland and Mr. Bellow's third grade classes have been studying fire safety. The classes have learned about the causes of most fires in the home. Mr. Bellow's class wrote a family fire drill for families of students at Ronald Johnson Elementary.

Ronald Johnson Elementary School Fire Safety

<u>Fire Safety Rules</u>

1. Never play with matches. <u>Remind</u> adults not to smoke in bed.

2. Do not plug too many electrical plugs into an <u>outlet</u>.

3. Know the sound your smoke detector makes when it detects smoke.

4. Make an <u>escape</u> plan for everyone to safely <u>exit</u> your home.

5. Practice crawling on the floor. The coolest temperatures are near the floor because heat rises.

6. Always touch doors before opening them. If they feel hot, find another way out.

7. Get out of the burning house quickly. Never stop to call the fire department first.

8. Never go back into a burning building. You can never tell where the fire might have spread.

9. Plan a meeting place for your family so you can know that everyone is safe.

10. Have a <u>schedule</u> for family fire drills. Practice different escape routes.

<u>Fire Safety Schedule</u>

January 10	Practice a fire drill. Exit through the front door.
February 10	Check the batteries in the smoke detector. If your house has more than one, be sure to check ALL of the smoke detectors.
March 10	Practice a fire drill. Exit through the back door.
April 10	Check the batteries in the smoke detector. If your house has more than one, be sure to check ALL of the smoke detectors.
May 10	Practice a fire drill. Choose an exit through a window in a bedroom.
June 10	Check the batteries in the smoke detector. If your house has more than one, be sure to check ALL of the smoke detectors.
July 10	Practice a fire drill. Exit through the front door.
August 10	Check the batteries in the smoke detector. If your house has more than one, be sure to check ALL of the smoke detectors.
September 10	Practice a fire drill. Pretend as if all doors are <u>blocked</u>.
October 10	Check the batteries in the smoke detector. If your house has more than one, be sure to check ALL of the smoke detectors.
November 10	Practice a fire drill. Pretend as if someone has swallowed too much

---

Common Core Standard RI.3.4

☐ In this story, the word <u>remind</u> means --

◯ help to remember

◯ obey

◯ order

◯ teach

Common Core Standard RI.3.4, Common Core Standard RL.3.4

☐ In this story, the word <u>swallowed</u> means --

◯ inhaled

◯ exhaled

◯ gulped

◯ eaten

Common Core Standard RI.3.4

☐ In this story, the word <u>unplug</u> means --

◯ repair

◯ remove

◯ electrical

◯ put into

Common Core Standard RI.3.4, Common Core Standard RL.3.4

☐ In this story, the word <u>outlet</u> means --

⬭ an opening through which electricity travels

⬭ a great deal of anger

⬭ an escape

⬭ wiring system

Common Core Standard RI.3.4, Common Core Standard RL.3.4

☐ In this story, the word <u>escape</u> means --

⬭ to avoid

⬭ many entrances

⬭ plan

⬭ way to get out

Common Core Standard RI.3.4, Common Core Standard RL.3.4

☐ In this story, the word <u>exit</u> means --

⬭ return

⬭ leave

⬭ move from

⬭ flee quickly

Name _____   Date_____

Common Core Standard RI.3.4, Common Core Standard RL.3.4

☐ In this story, the word <u>schedule</u> means --

○ catalog

○ timetable

○ list of events

○ list of games

Common Core Standard RI.3.4, Common Core Standard RL.3.4

☐ In this story, the word <u>socket</u> means --

○ electrical opening

○ Christmas lights

○ little sock

○ dangerous materials

Common Core Standard RI.3.4, Common Core Standard RL.3.4

☐ In this story, the word <u>blocked</u> means --

○ closed off

○ interruption

○ toy

○ piece of wood

Common Core Standard RL.3.2

☐ **Why is it important to plan a meeting place for the family?**

   ⬭ To have a long talk

   ⬭ To discuss the fire

   ⬭ To teach about fire safety

   ⬭ To make sure everyone is safe

Common Core Standard RI.3.4, Common Core Standard RL.3.4

☐ **During a fire the coolest place is near the floor because --**

   ⬭ the carpet is soft

   ⬭ the heat will rise to the top of the room

   ⬭ it is low

   ⬭ the air conditioning blows there

Common Core Standard RI.3.4, Common Core Standard RL.3.4

☐ **Why did Mr. Bellow's class write the family fire drill?**

   ⬭ It was an assignment.

   ⬭ Ms. Roland's class studied the cause of fires.

   ⬭ They had been studying fire safety.

   ⬭ The families did not have a fire drill.

Common Core Standard RI.3.3

☐ **What should be done the month before the batteries on the smoke detector are checked?**

◯ Purchase new batteries

◯ Practice a fire drill

◯ Go into the burning building

◯ Practice exiting through the back door

Common Core Standard RI.3.3

☐ **What should happen first before a door is opened in a burning house?**

◯ Touch the door

◯ Crawl on the floor to check the temperature

◯ Plan a family meeting place

◯ Make a schedule for practicing fire safety

Common Core Standard RI.3.3

☐ **What should happen first if the smoke detector sounds off?**

◯ Gather up favorite toys

◯ Call the fire station

◯ Look at the fire

◯ Get out of the burning building quickly

Common Core Standard RI.3.7

☐ The family fire safety drill rules were written –

⬭ at home

⬭ in Mr. Bellow's classroom

⬭ in Ms. Roland's classroom

⬭ at the fire station

Common Core Standard RI.3.7

☐ The family safety schedule was written to be used

⬭ at school

⬭ at a business

⬭ at Ronald Johnson Elementary

⬭ at a home

Common Core Standard RI.3.7, Common Core Standard RL.3.2

☐ According to the Fire Safety Rules, in which month should you practice a fire drill?

⬭ December

⬭ February

⬭ September

⬭ June

Common Core Standard RI.3.1, Common Core Standard RL.3.1

☐ **Where does the Fire Safety Schedule say to practice exiting on May 10th?**

⬯ The front door

⬯ The back door

⬯ A kitchen window

⬯ A bedroom window

Common Core Standard RI.3.1, Common Core Standard RL.3.1

☐ **The Fire Safety Schedule is a list of --**

⬯ things to remember

⬯ fire safety rules

⬯ activities for a family to do at home

⬯ homework that must be completed each month

Common Core Standard RI.3.1, Common Core Standard RL.3.1

☐ **What should happen on November 10th during the fire drill?**

⬯ Practice the fire drill

⬯ Pretend someone has swallowed too much smoke

⬯ Write an escape route

⬯ Check the wires on the Christmas tree

Common Core Standard RL.3.5

☐ **Which of these describes what happens in the first paragraph?**

⬭ What to do in case of a fire

⬭ Preventing wildfires

⬭ Two classes study fire safety

⬭ Creating fire drills for Black Elementary

Common Core Standard RI.3.1, Common Core Standard RL.3.2

☐ **What is the main idea of this story?**

⬭ Preventive steps for making certain students know what to do in case of a fire

⬭ Rules for students to follow to prevent a fire

⬭ Visiting a fire station to learn about fire safety

⬭ Remember to change the batteries in the smoke detector

Common Core Standard RL.3.5

☐ **What is the section "Fire Safety Schedule" mostly about?**

⬭ Rules for preventing fires

⬭ Family fire drills for 12 months

⬭ How to be prepared for a fire

⬭ Completing a smoke detector test each month

Common Core Standard RI.3.6

☐ What could be a problem if the batteries are not checked in a smoke detector?

    ◯ The owner would need to buy batteries.

    ◯ In case of a fire, the smoke detector might not work.

    ◯ The batteries could cause a fire.

    ◯ The owner would need to buy a new smoke detector.

Common Core Standard RI.3.6

☐ Why do the Fire Safety Rules say not to stop to call the fire department?

    ◯ It is more important to get out of the burning building first.

    ◯ The fire department would need directions to the fire.

    ◯ The telephone would be disconnected.

    ◯ The family would be waiting at the meeting place.

Common Core Standard RI.3.6

☐ Why does the Fire Safety Schedule say to unplug Christmas light cords at the wall socket?

    ◯ They use too much electricity.

    ◯ A bulb could burn out.

    ◯ The socket could be old.

    ◯ The wires will not catch the tree on fire if they are unplugged.

Common Core Standard RI.3.6

☐ Why is it dangerous for adults to smoke in bed?

    ◯ They might fall asleep while smoking.

    ◯ They might fall out of the bed.

    ◯ They might not remember to follow the safety rules.

    ◯ They might wake up too early.

Common Core Standard RI.3.6

☐ What could be a reason a smoke detector did not make any sound?

    ◯ New batteries

    ◯ Not following the Fire Safety Rules

    ◯ Old batteries

    ◯ Plugging too many electrical plugs into an outlet

Common Core Standard RI.3.6

☐ Information in the story suggests that if a family follows the Fire Safety Schedule they will –

    ◯ never have a fire

    ◯ know what to do if they ever have a fire in their home

    ◯ get an award from the fire department

    ◯ need to buy batteries

Common Core Standard RI.3.9, Common Core Standard RI.3.5

☐ **What is different about December 10th from most of the others on the Fire Safety Schedule?**

     ◯ It is not very important.

     ◯ It is easier to do.

     ◯ It is harder to do.

     ◯ It deals with Christmas decorations.

Common Core Standard RI.3.9, Common Core Standard RI.3.5

☐ **What is different about the fire safety practice on January 10th and March 10th?**

     ◯ The fire drill

     ◯ The escape route

     ◯ The kind of batteries used in the smoke detector

     ◯ The day of the month

Common Core Standard RI.3.9

☐ **What did Mr. Bellow's class do that Ms. Roland's class did not?**

     ◯ Wrote a family fire drill

     ◯ Studied fire safety

     ◯ Studied the causes of most fires

     ◯ Called the fire department

Common Core Standard RI.3.6

☐ **The Fire Safety Rules and the Fire Safety Schedule were probably written in –**

○ June

○ July

○ December

○ February

Common Core Standard RI.3.6

☐ **The schedule recommends to practice exiting through different doors because –**

○ the back door is the best place to exit

○ a fire can occur in any part of a house

○ everyone like to practice

○ a window is the best place to exit

Common Core Standard RI.3.6

☐ **Why is it not safe to plug too many electrical plugs into one outlet?**

○ The outlet might not work.

○ It will make everyone afraid.

○ The plugs might be old.

○ It could cause a fire.

Common Core Standard RL.3.3, Common Core Standard RL.3.6

☐ The reader can tell that Mr. Bellow's class --

⬭ liked fires

⬭ understood fire safety better than Ms. Roland's class

⬭ were eager to finish their study of fires

⬭ produced a fire safety plan that any family can use

Common Core Standard RI.3.7, Common Core Standard RL3.6

☐ Information in the story suggests that obeying the Fire Safety Rules should be done --

⬭ once a month

⬭ along with the Fire Safety Schedule

⬭ only by adults

⬭ only by Ronald Johnson Elementary families

Common Core Standard RI.3.3, Common Core Standard RL.3.6

☐ The Fire Safety Schedule says to check the smoke detector batteries every two months because --

⬭ the batteries can die at any time

⬭ the batteries cost a lot of money

⬭ it says to do it

⬭ the students wrote the plan

Common Core Standard RL.3.3, Common Core Standard RL.3.6

☐ **When the entire school received the School Fire Safety plan, Ms. Roland and Mr. Bellow's classes probably felt –**

◯ ashamed

◯ proud

◯ embarrassed

◯ annoyed

Common Core Standard RL.3.3, Common Core Standard RL.3.6

☐ **How would someone probably feel during a house fire?**

◯ Afraid

◯ Disappointed

◯ Enraged

◯ Cold

Common Core Standard RL.3.3, Common Core Standard RL.3.6

☐ **Practicing the Fire Safety Schedule should make someone feel --**

◯ trustworthy

◯ afraid

◯ friendly

◯ confident

Common Core Standard RI.3.6, Common Core Standard RI.3.7

☐ **Why do the Fire Safety Rules say never to go back into a burning building?**

○ The fire may have gone out.

○ You will get in the way of the firemen.

○ You do not know where the fire has spread.

○ The fire is very hot.

Common Core Standard RI.3.3, Common Core Standard RI.3.6

☐ **The Fire Safety Schedule says to check ALL of the smoke detectors because --**

○ it is important that all of them are working

○ a fire may start in the kitchen

○ the students thought it was a good idea

○ Mr. Bellow required it to say that

Common Core Standard RI.3.6, Common Core Standard RI.3.7

☐ **Why did the students write a Fire Safety Schedule?**

○ The firemen suggested that it would be a good idea.

○ Ms. Roland wanted her class to do the assignment.

○ All Fire Safety Rules must have a Fire Safety Schedule.

○ It is Step #10 in the Fire Safety Rules.

Common Core Standard RI.3.1, Common Core Standard RL.3.1

☐ **Which is a FACT in this story?**

⬭ Two classes at Ronald Johnson Elementary studied fire safety.

⬭ It is very dangerous for anyone to use matches.

⬭ The back door is the best exit in case of a fire.

⬭ It will take the firemen at least eight minutes to arrive at the burning building.

Common Core Standard RI.3.1, Common Core Standard RL.3.1

☐ **Which is a FACT in this story?**

⬭ The best way to save lives is to check the smoke detector.

⬭ Christmas lights are very dangerous.

⬭ Practicing a fire drill will allow you to escape unharmed.

⬭ Mr. Bellow's class wrote a family fire drill.

Common Core Standard RI.3.1, Common Core Standard RL.3.1

☐ **Which is an OPINION in this story?**

⬭ The third grade classes at Black Elementary have been studying fire safety.

⬭ Mr. Bellow and Ms. Roland are third grade teachers.

⬭ You should practice crawling on the floor during a fire drill.

⬭ The Fire Safety Schedule begins in January and ends in December.

What was it like to travel in a wagon?

The year was 1876 in Texas. Abigale and her family went on a trip to visit their grandparents. Because it was the first time Abigale had made the trip, she kept a diary of their adventures.

September 22

Today we got up very early to begin our trip to see Grandpa and Grandma Turner. Ma and Pa have said it will be a long and dusty journey. Ma brought some beef jerky and dried fruit for us to eat along the way. My brother, Nathan, and my sister, Rachel, think we may see Indians. Pa says most of the Indians are gone, but some are still living north of the Red River. He says they come into Texas to hunt for deer and buffalo. I hope they stay away from us. Pa gave us jobs to do on the trip. Pa will ride his horse in front of the wagon and make sure we follow the right trail. Ma's job is to drive the wagon team. Ma, Rachel, and I are going to ride in the wagon. My job is to care for Rachel. Rachel is too young for a job, but Pa told her to watch for rabbits. Nathan is going to walk in front of the wagon and pick up stones. This is an important job because a large rock could cause a wagon wheel to break or fall off. Nathan almost stepped on a rattlesnake. He thought it was a big stick lying near the road. When it coiled and began to rattle, Nathan hollered. Pa came riding back and shot the snake with his rifle. After a long day we made camp beneath some cottonwood trees near a small stream. I was so tired I fell asleep before Ma had finished washing the dishes.

September 23

We got up before sunrise to begin the second day of our journey. Today we traveled through the plains of Texas. Pa told us to watch for dust clouds because it could be Indians. I was really frightened. Nathan pointed out rabbits, a coyote, and a funny looking bird called a roadrunner to us. Before we stopped for lunch, we heard Pa shoot. Ma told us not to worry, but I could tell she was scared. Pa soon rode up with a deer draped across his horse. He said we would have fresh meat for supper. He and Nathan skinned the deer, and Pa put the deer in the wagon. All afternoon I thought about how good the deer meat would taste tonight. We built our camp near a small stream. The deer meat tasted as good as I thought it would. The coyotes must have smelled the meat because I heard them howling all night.

September 24

Today we arrived at Grandpa and Grandma's house. Grandma Turner had lots of good food for us to eat and a soft bed for me to sleep in. I do not have to worry about Indians or coyotes tonight. Grandma Turner had sugar cookies in the cookie jar for me. Grandpa Turner had a surprise for me. He gave me a pony. I named her "Stockings" because she has three white feet. Pa says we are going to stay for four days. I know I will have lots of fun.

Common Core Standard RI.3.4, Common Core Standard RL.3.4

☐ **In this story, the word <u>hollered</u> means --**

    ⬭ jumped

    ⬭ made a loud noise

    ⬭ ran for cover

    ⬭ cried

Common Core Standard RI.3.4

☐ **The word <u>traveled</u> in the story means --**

    ⬭ became famous

    ⬭ made pictures

    ⬭ showed

    ⬭ to go

Common Core Standard RI.3.4

☐ **In this story, the word <u>howling</u> means --**

    ⬭ crying loudly

    ⬭ eating

    ⬭ walking around

    ⬭ fighting

Common Core Standard RI.3.4

☐   In this story, the word <u>journey</u> means --

◯   came near

◯   a place to keep horses

◯   long trip

◯   picnic

Common Core Standard RI.3.4, Common Core Standard RL.3.4

☐   In this story, the word <u>jerky</u> means --

◯   quick movement

◯   food

◯   falling

◯   hopping

Common Core Standard RI.3.4, Common Core Standard RL.3.4

☐   The word <u>draped</u> means --

◯   curtain

◯   piece of cloth

◯   killed

◯   thrown over

Common Core Standard RI.3.4, Common Core Standard RL.3.4

☐ **In this story, the word <u>coiled</u> means –**

⬭ a piece of wire

⬭ stretched out

⬭ ran away

⬭ made the shape of a circle

Common Core Standard RI.3.4, Common Core Standard RL.3.4

☐ **The word <u>rattle</u> in this story means --**

⬭ a baby's toy

⬭ short, fast sounds

⬭ looking at

⬭ hurries

Common Core Standard RI.3.4, Common Core Standard RL.3.4

☐ **The word <u>beneath</u> in the story means --**

⬭ across from

⬭ beside

⬭ below

⬭ above

Common Core Standard RI.3.7

☐ How did Abigale travel to see their grandparents?

⬭ Walked

⬭ Wagon

⬭ Stagecoach

⬭ Horse

Common Core Standard RI.3.3

☐ Why did Pa think they would not see any Indians?

⬭ The Indians were afraid of Pa.

⬭ Indians like to hunt at night.

⬭ Grandpa said there were no Indians in Texas.

⬭ Most of the Indians had moved away.

Common Core Standard RI.3.1

☐ Abigale helped Ma --

⬭ bake cookies

⬭ skin the deer

⬭ care for Rachel

⬭ watch for rabbits

Common Core Standard RI.3.8

☐ **Which of these happened last?**

◯ Pa skinned the deer.

◯ Pa put the deer in the wagon.

◯ We ate lunch.

◯ We heard a shot.

Common Core Standard RI.3.8

☐ **Which of these happened first?**

◯ Nathan walked in front of the wagon.

◯ Pa shot the snake.

◯ We heard Nathan yell.

◯ The snake began to rattle.

Common Core Standard RI.3.3

☐ **When did Abigale arrive at her grandparents?**

◯ The first day

◯ The third day

◯ The second day

◯ The next day

Common Core Standard RI.3.7

☐ Which of these events happened on September 23?

- ⬭ The snake coiled and rattled.

- ⬭ Abigale ate sugar cookies.

- ⬭ They built their camp beneath cottonwood trees.

- ⬭ They watched for dust clouds.

Common Core Standard RI.3.3

☐ What happened after Pa and Nathan skinned the deer?

- ⬭ Nathan showed us a funny looking bird.

- ⬭ The coyotes howled during the night.

- ⬭ Ma was afraid when she heard the shot.

- ⬭ Pa gave us jobs to do on the trip.

Common Core Standard RI.3.1, Common Core Standard RI.3.3

☐ According to the story, what was the first animal Nathan saw?

- ⬭ Roadrunner

- ⬭ Coyote

- ⬭ Snake

- ⬭ Rabbit

Common Core Standard RL.3.7

☐ **Where did most of the story take place?**

- ⬭ On the trail
- ⬭ Near the stream
- ⬭ At Grandpa Turner's ranch
- ⬭ Beside the Red River

Common Core Standard RL.3.7

☐ **Where is the diary being written?**

- ⬭ At the ranch
- ⬭ On a horse
- ⬭ On the journey
- ⬭ At home

Common Core Standard RL.3.7

☐ **Abigale and her family camped each night –**

- ⬭ On the Red River
- ⬭ At Grandma Turner's ranch
- ⬭ Under the cottonwood trees
- ⬭ Near a stream

Common Core Standard RI.3.7

☐ **What state is found to the north of Texas?**

○ Louisiana

○ Arkansas

○ Oklahoma

○ Texas

Common Core Standard RI.3.7

☐ **Which state is the city of Oklahoma City located in?**

○ Texas

○ Oklahoma

○ Arkansas

○ Louisiana

Common Core Standard RI.3.7

☐ **According to the maps, which city is closer to Abigale's home?**

○ Ft. Worth

○ Houston

○ Oklahoma City

○ San Antonio

Common Core Standard RI.3.2

☐ **What is the main idea of this story?**

⬭ The visit with Grandma and Grandpa Turner will be fun.

⬭ In 1876 a family went to visit their grandparents.

⬭ The Indians might attack their wagon.

⬭ Pa killed a deer.

Common Core Standard RI.3.1, Common Core Standard RL.3.5

☐ **What is the last paragraph of the diary mostly about?**

⬭ Getting a pony

⬭ Traveling on the plains of Texas

⬭ Arriving at Grandma and Grandpa Turner's ranch

⬭ Beginning the trip

Common Core Standard RI.3.1, Common Core Standard RL.3.5

☐ **What is the main idea of the first part of the diary?**

⬭ The first day of the journey

⬭ Eating the deer

⬭ Naming the pony "Stockings"

⬭ Killing a snake

Common Core Standard RI.3.1, Common Core Standard RL.3.1

☐ This story is mainly about a girl who –

○ gets a new pony

○ is afraid of Indians

○ travels with her family to see her grandparents

○ sees many animals

Common Core Standard RI.3.2, Common Core Standard RL.3.5

☐ Which sentence tells what this story is mostly about?

○ Each family member had an important job on the trip.

○ A girl and her family make a trip in 1876.

○ The Indians were a threat on the trip.

○ Pa killed and skinned a deer for food.

Common Core Standard RI.3.2, Common Core Standard RL.3.2

☐ The main idea of this story is that –

○ Nathan had the most important job

○ food was scarce

○ the children learned about animals

○ a family made a trip to their grandparents

Common Core Standard RI.3.8, Common Core Standard RL.3.6

☐ **What could be a problem if Nathan did not do his job?**

⬭ The wagon would go very slowly.

⬭ Nathan would not be allowed to eat supper.

⬭ A wheel could break on the wagon.

⬭ Pa would need to ride in the wagon.

Common Core Standard RI.3.8, Common Core Standard RL.3.6

☐ **What problem could the family have if they saw Indians?**

⬭ The Indians could scare off the animals.

⬭ The Indians could take their food.

⬭ No problem

⬭ The Indians would go to visit their grandparents.

Common Core Standard RI.3.8, Common Core Standard RL.3.6

☐ **When they heard Pa shoot his rifle, what could have been the problem?**

⬭ Pa was hungry.

⬭ Pa wanted Ma to hurry.

⬭ Pa was happy.

⬭ Pa could have seen Indians.

Common Core Standard RI.3.8

☐ **Abigale's family built camp near a stream each night because --**

◯ Rachel liked to play in the water

◯ the streams were pretty

◯ they were near the cottonwood trees

◯ they needed water for drinking and cooking

Common Core Standard RI.3.8, Common Core Standard RL.3.3

☐ **Abilgale did not worry about coyotes when she arrived at Grandpa Turner's house because --**

◯ they had gone away

◯ she slept in a bed inside the house

◯ Pa had a rifle

◯ the coyotes were not hungry

Common Core Standard RI.3.8

☐ **Abigale had fresh meat for supper on September 23rd because --**

◯ the Indians shared their food

◯ Nathan spotted a rabbit

◯ Pa killed a deer on the trail

◯ Ma brought food from home

Common Core Standard RI.3.3, Common Core Standard RL.3.3

☐ **Ma was worried about Pa when she heard him shoot because --**

- ⬯ it could mean danger for the family
- ⬯ Pa was a poor shot with the rifle
- ⬯ Nathan had seen Indians
- ⬯ it was going to be a long journey

Common Core Standard RI.3.3, Common Core Standard RL.3.6

☐ **Why did Ma bring food on the trip?**

- ⬯ She was unhappy.
- ⬯ She liked to cook.
- ⬯ They might not find any game to kill for food.
- ⬯ She was afraid of Indians.

Common Core Standard RI.3.3, Common Core Standard RL.3.6

☐ **Pa gave Rachel the job of watching for rabbits because he --**

- ⬯ liked rabbits
- ⬯ wanted her to have a job like everyone else
- ⬯ knew there were no rabbits
- ⬯ knew Indians needed the rabbits for food

Common Core Standard RI.3.3

☐ Abigale was given the job of caring for Rachel because --

◯ they were both girls

◯ Abigale was older than Rachel

◯ Nathan did not like girls

◯ Pa rode his horse

Common Core Standard RI.3.3, Common Core Standard RL.3.3

☐ Nathan and Abigale were given important jobs because they both were --

◯ in charge of cooking the food

◯ eager to make the trip

◯ afraid of Indians

◯ older and could be trusted to do a good job

Common Core Standard RI.3.3, Common Core Standard RL.3.3

☐ On the trip Pa and Ma were --

◯ prepared for unexpected events

◯ afraid

◯ glad to leave their home

◯ tired

Common Core Standard RL.3.6

☐ **You can tell from this story that travel in 1876 --**

    ⬭ made people sick

    ⬭ was safe

    ⬭ could be dangerous

    ⬭ did not go slowly

Common Core Standard RL.3.6

☐ **Abigale's family did not --**

    ⬭ help each other on the journey

    ⬭ travel to see their grandparents very often

    ⬭ earn much money

    ⬭ like fresh deer meat

Common Core Standard RL.3.6

☐ **People who lived in Texas in 1876 --**

    ⬭ did not have an easy life

    ⬭ lived in small towns

    ⬭ killed all of the animals

    ⬭ liked to fight Indians

Common Core Standard RI.3.3, Common Core Standard RL.3.3

☐ **We know the snake frightened Nathan because --**

⬭ he picked up stones

⬭ he walked in front of the wagon

⬭ he thought it was a stick

⬭ he yelled

Common Core Standard RI.3.3, Common Core Standard RL.3.3

☐ **Abigale probably know her mother was worried when she heard Pa shoot because --**

⬭ Ma was happy

⬭ Ma was angry

⬭ she had seen Ma look worried before

⬭ Ma began to cook supper

Common Core Standard RI.3.3

☐ **Pa told Ma, Abigale, and Rachel to ride in the wagon because he knew that --**

⬭ walking or riding a horse would be too tiring

⬭ Nathan wanted to walk

⬭ they did not have any shoes

⬭ Pa did not like to ride in a wagon

Common Core Standard RL.3.3, Common Core Standard RL.3.6

☐ On the second night of the journey Abigale probably felt afraid because –

◯ Pa had killed a deer

◯ the coyotes were near their camp

◯ Indians were looking for food

◯ Ma had been worried

Common Core Standard RL.3.3, Common Core Standard RL.3.6

☐ How did Abigale probably feel the night before they went on the trip?

◯ Friendly

◯ Surprised

◯ Angry

◯ Excited

Common Core Standard RL.3.3, Common Core Standard RL.3.6

☐ How did Abigale feel at the end of the diary?

◯ Frightened

◯ Strange

◯ Thankful

◯ Curious

Common Core Standard RI.3.7, Common Core Standard RL.3.5

☐ **According to the map at the bottom of the page, Abigale and her family traveled in which state?**

⬭ Arkansas

⬭ Texas

⬭ Oklahoma

⬭ Louisiana

Common Core Standard RI.3.7, Common Core Standard RL.3.5

☐ **According to the map at the bottom of the page, what town did Abigale travel through?**

⬭ Houston

⬭ Abilene

⬭ Fort Worth

⬭ None

Common Core Standard RI.3.7

☐ **Look at the map. Which of the following statements is true?**

⬭ Abigale and her family traveled on a freeway.

⬭ They traveled in the desert.

⬭ Towns were very far apart.

⬭ They traveled over mountains.

Common Core Standard RI.3.1, Common Core Standard RL.3.1

☐ **In this story, which of these is NOT a fact?**

◯ Abigale was afraid of Indians.

◯ Grandpa Turner wanted to surprise Abigale.

◯ Nathan shot a deer for supper.

◯ Ma knew how to drive the wagon.

Common Core Standard RI.3.1, Common Core Standard RL.3.1

☐ **Which of these is an OPINION from the story?**

◯ It took them three days to arrive at their grandparents' house.

◯ The coyotes smelled the fresh deer meat.

◯ In 1876 travel in Texas was dangerous.

◯ Abigale had not been to see her grandparents.

Common Core Standard RI.3.1, Common Core Standard RL.3.1

☐ **Which is a FACT in the story?**

◯ Nathan yelled when he saw the snake.

◯ Pa chased the deer before he shot it.

◯ Ma and Pa thought the trip would be easy.

◯ Indians come into Texas to rob banks.

Teeth — what do they really do?

Humans and animals have different kinds of teeth. Teeth are the body's hardest, most <u>durable</u> organ. Human and animal teeth have been found that are over a thousand years old.

Humans

Humans use their teeth to tear, grind, and chew food. Each tooth does a different kind of job. Teeth help humans form words and also give support to the face muscles so they can smile.

Adult humans have 32 teeth, 16 in the upper jaw and 16 in the lower jaw. The teeth on the right side of the jaw are <u>identical</u> to the teeth on the left side. These matching teeth on opposite sides are called sets or pairs.

Human teeth are different sizes and shapes. Humans have 4 kinds of teeth. The incisors are sharp and are used to cut food. The canines, or eyeteeth, tear food. Behind the canines are the bicuspids, or <u>premolars</u>, where chewing happens. The molars are often called wisdom teeth. They were used thousands of years ago when humans needed extra chewing and grinding power because they ate raw foods. Today wisdom teeth are not needed, so many humans have them taken out.

Humans have 2 sets of teeth during their lives. The first set of teeth is called the "baby teeth." When a child is about 6 years old, another set of larger teeth, called <u>permanent</u> teeth, begins to push the first set of teeth out of the gums. Then for about 7 years the permanent teeth take the place of the "baby teeth" in a human's mouth. The permanent teeth should last the <u>remainder</u> of a human's life.

Animals

Most animals use their teeth to chew their food and do other jobs. For example, tigers have long, sharp teeth for killing their <u>prey</u>, and beavers have <u>chisel-like</u> teeth that they use to cut down large trees for building dams.

The teeth of animals are the same size and shape. Mammals have teeth that allow them to catch, chew, and digest food. Animals that eat only insects have square teeth that help them to grind the hard shells of insects. Dogs and cats have large teeth that help them fight. Horses, cows, and deer eat only plants, so their teeth are sharp.

Some animals only have one set of teeth during their lives. These teeth continue to grow throughout an animal's life. These animals wear their teeth down because they <u>gnaw</u>. If they did not gnaw, their teeth would be very long. For example, the teeth of a beaver can grow up to 4 feet a year.

Reptiles

Some reptiles have teeth. Snakes have an egg tooth that helps the young snake to chip its way out of the egg. Many reptiles have teeth growing on their tongue or the top of their mouth, and some have a second set of teeth in their throat. Some snakes, such as rattlesnakes, have large <u>fangs</u> that deliver venom to their victims.

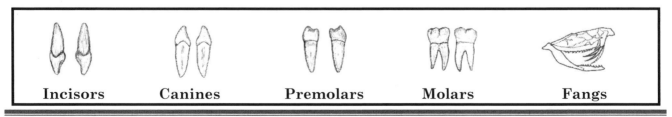

| Incisors | Canines | Premolars | Molars | Fangs |

62

Common Core Standard RI.3.4

☐ In this story, the word <u>durable</u> means --

◯ hard

◯ white

◯ long lasting

◯ important

Common Core Standard RI.3.4

☐ In this story, the word <u>premolars</u> means --

◯ teeth used for chewing

◯ baby teeth

◯ dark areas found on the body

◯ animal teeth

Common Core Standard RI.3.4

☐ In this story, the word <u>remainder</u> means --

◯ part of

◯ number in a division problem

◯ adult teeth

◯ rest of

Name _____   Date_____

Common Core Standard RI.3.4, Common Core Standard RL.3.4

☐ **In this story, the words <u>chisel-like</u> mean --**

⬭ common

⬭ unusual

⬭ white

⬭ sharp on the edges

Common Core Standard RI.3.4

☐ **In this story, the word <u>gnaw</u> means --**

⬭ grow

⬭ chew

⬭ know

⬭ eat

Common Core Standard RI.3.4

☐ **In this story, the word <u>fangs</u> means --**

⬭ filled with poison

⬭ small

⬭ large teeth

⬭ deadly teeth

Common Core Standard RI.3.4

☐ **In this story, the word <u>identical</u> means --**

- ⬭ the same
- ⬭ very different
- ⬭ twins
- ⬭ on the other side

Common Core Standard RI.3.4

☐ **In this story, the word <u>permanent</u> means --**

- ⬭ lasting for seven years
- ⬭ lasting forever
- ⬭ coming in
- ⬭ baby teeth

Common Core Standard RI.3.4, Common Core Standard RL.3.4

☐ **In this story, the word <u>prey</u> means --**

- ⬭ small animals
- ⬭ reptiles
- ⬭ enemies
- ⬭ victim

Common Core Standard RI.3.1

☐ Why are teeth important to a human when they talk?

     ⬭ Teeth help people smile.

     ⬭ Teeth help people form words.

     ⬭ Teeth are different sizes and shapes.

     ⬭ Teeth have different kinds of jobs.

Common Core Standard RI.3.1

☐ According to the story, which animal has only one set of teeth during their life?

     ⬭ Mammals

     ⬭ Dogs and cats

     ⬭ Reptiles

     ⬭ Beaver

Common Core Standard RI.3.1

☐ Based on information in the story, when do most humans begin to lose their first set of teeth?

     ⬭ About 6 years of age

     ⬭ About 8 years of age

     ⬭ About 5 years of age

     ⬭ Never

Common Core Standard RI.3.5

☐ **How many teeth do human adults have?**

⬭ 16

⬭ 32

⬭ 24

⬭ 7

Common Core Standard RI.3.5

☐ **What shape are the teeth of animals that eat only insects?**

⬭ Teeth

⬭ Long and sharp

⬭ Fangs

⬭ Square

Common Core Standard RI.3.5

☐ **The oldest human and animal teeth that have been found are --**

⬭ over a thousand years old

⬭ shaped like a square

⬭ do not contain wisdom teeth

⬭ are all the same size

Common Core Standard RI.3.3

☐ **What is used for chewing before the permanent teeth come in?**

○ Small bites

○ Premolars

○ Baby teeth

○ Wisdom teeth

Common Core Standard RI.3.3

☐ **What does a rattlesnake use to kill its prey after it catches it?**

○ Teeth

○ Egg Tooth

○ Tongue

○ Fangs

Common Core Standard RI.3.3

☐ **After animals spend a lot of time chewing, they --**

○ wear their teeth down

○ lose their teeth

○ fall asleep

○ get new teeth

Common Core Standard RI.3.3, Common Core Standard RL.3.3

☐ **Horses and deer need to live near plants because they --**

- ⬭ like to hide in plants from their enemies

- ⬭ use plants for food

- ⬭ have square shaped teeth

- ⬭ have only one set of teeth

Common Core Standard RI.3.7

☐ **Where would bicuspids be found in a human's mouth?**

- ⬭ Next to the premolars

- ⬭ In front of the canines

- ⬭ Behind the premolars

- ⬭ Behind the canines

Common Core Standard RI.3.7

☐ **Beavers need to live near --**

- ⬭ swimming pools

- ⬭ a desert

- ⬭ large trees

- ⬭ cities

Common Core Standard RL.3.5

☐ **What is paragraph three mostly about?**

◯ The location of animals' teeth

◯ How animals catch their prey

◯ The number of human teeth

◯ The role of different kinds of teeth in a human's mouth

Common Core Standard RI.3.5, Common Core Standard RL.3.5

☐ **What is the main idea of paragraph eight?**

◯ Beavers grow very large teeth.

◯ Reptiles have teeth.

◯ Animals use their teeth to grind their food.

◯ Some animals grow very long teeth.

Common Core Standard RI.3.2

☐ **What is the main idea of this story?**

◯ Teeth are very important to humans, animals, and reptiles.

◯ Humans, animals, and reptiles like their teeth.

◯ Human get their first teeth when they are young.

◯ There could be many different problems if animals did not use their teeth.

Common Core Standard RI.3.6, Common Core Standard RI.3.8

☐ **The beaver would have a problem if he --**

◯ was surrounded by too many trees

◯ did not chew or gnaw most of the time

◯ was separated from his mother

◯ caught his prey

Common Core Standard RI.3.6, Common Core Standard RI.3.8

☐ **What would be the main problem for humans if the permanent teeth did not push out the baby teeth?**

◯ Not enough teeth

◯ Too many wisdom teeth

◯ Could not eat

◯ Too many teeth

Common Core Standard RI.3.6, Common Core Standard RI.3.8

☐ **What could be a problem if a person did not have any teeth?**

◯ They would not be able to drink anything.

◯ They could not eat.

◯ They would have difficulty talking.

◯ They could not use their computer.

Common Core Standard RI.3.3

☐ Horses have very sharp teeth because they –

⬭ eat plants

⬭ eat meat

⬭ bite people who are mistreating them

⬭ are well worn

Common Core Standard RI.3.3

☐ Animals that only eat insects have special teeth because they –

⬭ fly around

⬭ eat snails

⬭ grind food that is hard

⬭ are mammals

Common Core Standard RI.3.3

☐ Snakes have an egg tooth because --

⬭ they have fangs

⬭ it helps them to get out of the egg

⬭ it grows on their tongue

⬭ they have teeth

Common Core Standard RI.3.3

☐ **Rattlesnakes have fangs because they –**

⬭ are mean

⬭ are reptiles

⬭ are scary

⬭ use them to poison their victims

Common Core Standard RI.3.3

☐ **Human incisors are sharp because they –**

⬭ cut food

⬭ chew food

⬭ find food

⬭ tear food

Common Core Standard RI.3.1, Common Core Standard RI.3.3

☐ **Very old teeth from animals and humans have been found because teeth are –**

⬭ easily seen

⬭ easily found

⬭ long lasting

⬭ important to keep

Common Core Standard RI.3.9

☐ **How are human teeth different from animal teeth?**

◯ Human teeth are different sizes and shapes.

◯ Human teeth are white.

◯ Human teeth are sharp.

◯ Human teeth are used for chewing.

Common Core Standard RI.3.9

☐ **How are human teeth and animal teeth alike?**

◯ They have baby teeth.

◯ They have 32 teeth.

◯ They have an egg tooth.

◯ They can last a very long time.

Common Core Standard RI.3.9

☐ **How are human teeth on the right side of the mouth like teeth on the left side?**

◯ There are 32 on each side of the jaw.

◯ There are 16 on each side of the jaw.

◯ They are all wisdom teeth.

◯ They are all premolars.

Common Core Standard RI.3.6

☐ **If humans did not have canine teeth, they would probably –**

⬭ be able to eat faster

⬭ have difficulty eating

⬭ have fewer teeth to brush

⬭ not be able to talk

Common Core Standard RI.3.6

☐ **When a human has lost all of the baby teeth, they probably –**

⬭ have no teeth

⬭ are unable to smile

⬭ are about 13 years old

⬭ are 6 years old

Common Core Standard RI.3.6

☐ **Where would a person probably go to have wisdom teeth removed?**

⬭ To a dentist's office

⬭ To a doctor's office

⬭ To school

⬭ To the mall

Common Core Standard RI.3.3

☐ **Many humans have their wisdom teeth removed because they --**

⬯ are over a thousand years old

⬯ are too large

⬯ are no longer needed to grind food

⬯ cause pain

Common Core Standard RI.3.3

☐ **Animals do not have baby teeth because they --**

⬯ have an egg tooth

⬯ have one set of teeth

⬯ have teeth that are the same size and shape

⬯ use their teeth for killing their prey

Common Core Standard RI.3.3, Common Core Standard RI.3.6

☐ **Humans should take care of their teeth because they --**

⬯ grow new teeth every year

⬯ have 32 teeth

⬯ have wisdom teeth

⬯ use them every day

Common Core Standard RI.3.9

☐ How have human teeth changed over the years?

⬭ There are now have 32 teeth.

⬭ Wisdom teeth are no longer needed.

⬭ Baby teeth are not needed today.

⬭ Permanent teeth last for 50 years.

Common Core Standard RI.3.9

☐ How are most animal teeth alike?

⬭ Most animals use their teeth for building dams.

⬭ Most animals have long sharp teeth.

⬭ Most animals grind their food.

⬭ Most animals use their teeth for chewing their food.

Common Core Standard RI.3.9

☐ Long ago, how did animals and humans use their teeth in the same way?

⬭ They used their teeth to chip their way out of the egg.

⬭ They used their teeth to kill their prey.

⬭ They used their teeth to chew and grind raw foods.

⬭ They used their teeth to smile.

Common Core Standard RI.3.1, Common Core Standard RL.3.1

☐ **Which is a FACT in this story?**

○ Human teeth are important for communicating, smiling, and eating.

○ Some crafty animals, like the beavers, use their teeth to create shelter.

○ It is important to brush your teeth daily, so that they will last throughout your life.

○ Human teeth are used to tear, grind, and chew food.

Common Core Standard RI.3.1, Common Core Standard RL.3.1

☐ **Which is an OPINION in this story?**

○ Today wisdom teeth are not needed.

○ Chewing happens behind the canines.

○ Some reptiles have teeth.

○ Human teeth can last over a thousand years.

Common Core Standard RI.3.1, Common Core Standard RL.3.1

☐ **Which is a FACT in this story?**

○ Teeth are not the hardest organ in the body.

○ Humans have 32 sets of teeth.

○ Humans and animals have different kinds of teeth.

○ Incisors are used to tear food.

Smart Reptiles

Crocodiles are the largest and smartest living reptiles. The crocodile's brain is about the size of a hotdog. We know that crocodiles can learn because they can <u>recognize</u> a pattern when animals come to the river to drink at the same time each day. Therefore, it is not safe to <u>return</u> to the water at the same place at the same time every day where crocodiles live. You could end up as a crocodile snack.

In 1975 the American crocodile was put on the <u>endangered</u> species list. That means those animals are protected by the U.S. government. Crocodiles live only in Florida. <u>Experts</u> say that it is important to save crocodiles and to understand them.

Crocodiles live in and near water. Some people are worried because the number of crocodiles keeps growing. They worry because some crocodiles have been seen near people's homes or on the golf courses in Florida. A crocodile will attack just about anything that goes near the water, but usually eats fish, turtles, small animals, and birds. However, that does not mean humans are safe. Although no one has been attacked by a crocodile in over 51 years, their size and <u>strength</u> makes them very dangerous.

Mother crocodiles <u>guard</u> their nests and protect their young until they are about two years old. Crocodile mothers not only watch their nests, but also the nests of other mother crocodiles. They carry their babies in their mouths to protect them from enemies. Even with their care,

only about one out of every ten crocodile babies grow to be adults. The way they live and work as a <u>member</u> of a group shows how smart they are. The fact that they have lived since the age of the dinosaurs proves they can <u>adapt</u> to their environment.

Another reptile that is a close <u>relative</u> of a crocodile is the alligator. The word *alligator* came from the Spanish word for lizard, "*el largato.*" If you say it fast, it sounds like you are saying alligator. There are more alligators than crocodiles. There may be as many as 1 1/2 million alligators in Florida. Unlike crocodiles, alligators can be found in some southern states.

Alligators are also protected by the U.S. government. At one time they were killed for their skins, so the government had to protect the alligators from hunters. There are now alligator farms in Florida and Louisiana. On the farms the reptiles are fed often and kept in very warm, dark rooms. This <u>enables</u> them to grow quickly. These alligators are used for food and for other products.

Mother alligators build large, mound-shaped nests of mud and plants, where they lay their eggs. The mother stays near the nest to protect it from enemies. When ready to <u>hatch</u>, the young alligators grunt from inside their eggs, and their mother digs to open the nest. She may even help break the eggs open. Like the crocodile, the mother alligator also carries her young in her mouth to the water

ALLIGATOR or CROCODILE?	
<u>Alligator</u>	<u>Crocodile</u>
* can be up to 19 feet long	* can be up to 18 feet long
* are about 9 inches long when born	* are about 9 inches long when born
* have broad, flat <u>snouts</u>	* have long, thin snouts
* have no teeth showing when the mouth is closed	* have teeth that show when the mouth is closed
* build their nests above the ground	* build their nests below the ground

Common Core Standard RI.3.4

☐ **In this story, the word <u>endangered</u> means --**

    ◯ dangerous

    ◯ at risk

    ◯ living

    ◯ special

Common Core Standard RI.3.4

☐ **In this story, the word <u>enables</u> means --**

    ◯ allows

    ◯ find

    ◯ believe

    ◯ follow

Common Core Standard RI.3.4, Common Core Standard RL.3.4

☐ **In this story, the word <u>return</u> means --**

    ◯ stay away from

    ◯ follow quickly

    ◯ watch

    ◯ go back to

Common Core Standard RI.3.4, Common Core Standard RL.3.4

☐ **In this story, the word <u>recognize</u> means --**

   ⬭ to be seen

   ⬭ put together

   ⬭ create

   ⬭ identify

Common Core Standard RI.3.4

☐ **In this story, the word <u>experts</u> means --**

   ⬭ adults

   ⬭ people with a lot of knowledge

   ⬭ teenagers

   ⬭ information

Common Core Standard RI.3.4

☐ **In this story, the word <u>strength</u> means --**

   ⬭ weak

   ⬭ dangerous

   ⬭ strong

   ⬭ angry

Common Core Standard RI 3.4

☐ In this story, the word <u>member</u> means --

◯ part of

◯ trying to be friendly

◯ a large family

◯ intelligent

Common Core Standard RI.3.4, Common Core Standard RL.3.4

☐ In this story, the word <u>adapt</u> means --

◯ hard work

◯ get along with

◯ make fit

◯ not living

Common Core Standard RI.3.4, Common Core Standard RL.3.4

☐ In this story, the word <u>snouts</u> means --

◯ bodies

◯ noses

◯ mouths

◯ skin

Common Core Standard RI.3.4, Common Core Standard RL.3.4

☐ **In this story, the word <u>hatch</u> means –**

⬭ a small door or opening

⬭ opening in the deck of a ship

⬭ to be born

⬭ making loud noises

Common Core Standard RI.3.4, Common Core Standard RL.3.4

☐ **In this story, the word <u>relative</u> means –**

⬭ family member

⬭ friend

⬭ cousin

⬭ reptile

Common Core Standard RI.3.4, Common Core Standard RL.3.4 –

☐ **In this story, the word <u>guard</u> means**

⬭ build

⬭ sleep on

⬭ carry

⬭ watch over

Common Core Standard RI3.7

☐ **Crocodiles can only be found living in –**

   ⬭ swamps

   ⬭ Texas

   ⬭ small lakes

   ⬭ Florida

Common Core Standard RI3.4, Common Core Standard RI.3.5

☐ **What does the Spanish word for alligator mean?**

   ⬭ Crocodile

   ⬭ Lizard

   ⬭ El largato

   ⬭ Reptile

Common Core Standard RI3.7

☐ **About how many alligators live in Florida?**

   ⬭ 2 million

   ⬭ 2.5 million

   ⬭ 1.5 million

   ⬭ 1 million

Common Core Standard RI.3.3

☐ **What does a mother alligator do before she lays her eggs?**

◯ Searches for food

◯ Builds a large nest

◯ Helps break open the eggs

◯ Gives birth

Common Core Standard RI.3.3, Common Core Standard RL.3.3

☐ **After a crocodile knows that an animal is returning to the same place each day to get water or food, the crocodile**

◯ moves to another place

◯ moves her babies to safety

◯ builds a nest

◯ will probably attack the animal

Common Core Standard RI.3.3

☐ **Before the young alligators hatch, they**

◯ make a noise from inside the egg

◯ swim in the water

◯ dig to open the nest

◯ eat fish, turtles, and birds

Common Core Standard RI.3.3

☐ **Crocodiles live in or near --**

◯ ponds

◯ forests

◯ alligator farms

◯ golf courses

Common Core Standard RI.3.7

☐ **Where can alligator farms be found?**

◯ In the country

◯ Texas

◯ Louisiana

◯ Near the ocean

Common Core Standard RI.3.7

☐ **Which is a place where alligators probably would NOT be found?**

◯ Texas

◯ New York

◯ Near water

◯ Louisiana

Common Core Standard RI.3.7, Common Core Standard RL.3.9

☐ **An adult crocodile could grow to be --**

⬭ 19 feet

⬭ 9 inches

⬭ 9 feet

⬭ 18 feet

Common Core Standard RI.3.7, Common Core Standard RL.3.9

☐ **An alligator's snout is --**

⬭ long and thin

⬭ wide and flat

⬭ long and smooth

⬭ short and flat

Common Core Standard RI.3.7, Common Core Standard RL.3.9

☐ **The crocodile builds a nest**

⬭ above the ground

⬭ near a farm

⬭ below the ground

⬭ in the water

Common Core Standard RI.3.2, Common Core Standard RL.3.2

☐ **What is this story mostly about?**

◯ Alligators and crocodiles live in Florida and Louisiana and are very dangerous to humans.

◯ Mother alligators and crocodiles use mud and plants to build their nests above the ground.

◯ Alligators and crocodiles are alike in many ways, but also have many differences.

◯ When the young alligators are ready to hatch, they dig open the nest and run to the water.

Common Core Standard RI.3.2, Common Core Standard RL.3.2

☐ **What is the main idea of this story?**

◯ Where crocodiles can be found

◯ Where alligators can be found

◯ How alligators and crocodiles get along together

◯ How alligators and crocodiles are alike and different

Common Core Standard RL.3.5

☐ **What is the main idea of paragraph three?**

◯ How crocodiles can be dangerous to humans and animals

◯ How crocodiles live

◯ What crocodiles like to eat

◯ How mother crocodiles guard their nests

Common Core Standard RI.3.6, Common Core Standard RL.3.6

☐ **What could have happened if the United States government had not started protecting crocodiles?**

○ There would have been too many crocodiles.

○ There probably would not be any crocodiles living today.

○ There might have been too many alligators.

○ Hunters would have paid fines for killing crocodiles.

Common Core Standard RI.3.6, Common Core Standard RL.3.6

☐ **A human or an animal could have a problem with a crocodile if they -**

○ moved to a golf course

○ lived in Louisiana

○ owned an alligator farm

○ went to the same place at the same time each day to go swimming in the river

Common Core Standard RI.3.6, Common Core Standard RL.3.6

☐ **What could be a problem if all of the crocodile babies grew to be adult crocodiles?**

○ There would be too many crocodiles.

○ The crocodiles would move to Louisiana.

○ Mother alligators would not need to guard their babies.

○ Mother crocodiles could build their nests above the ground.

Common Core Standard RI.3.3

☐ Alligators raised on farms are kept in very warm, dark rooms because they --

   ◯ are not healthy

   ◯ are dangerous

   ◯ are expensive

   ◯ will grow very quickly

Common Core Standard RI.3.3

☐ We know that crocodiles can learn because they --

   ◯ have feelings

   ◯ are reptiles

   ◯ can recognize patterns

   ◯ are smart

Common Core Standard RI.3.3

☐ Young alligators make a noise inside their eggs because they are --

   ◯ hungry

   ◯ ready to hatch

   ◯ going in the water

   ◯ laying their eggs

Common Core Standard RI.3.6, Common Core Standard RL.3.3

☐ **If a crocodile is disturbed, it will probably --**

◯ be angry

◯ attack

◯ swim away

◯ send a warning to other crocodiles

Common Core Standard RI.3.6, Common Core Standard RL.3.3

☐ **If a young crocodile or alligator was separated from its mother at a very young age, it would most likely --**

◯ find its father

◯ move to an alligator farm

◯ find another mother

◯ die

Common Core Standard RI.3.6, Common Core Standard RL.3.3

☐ **If a young alligator is unable to get out of its egg, it will probably --**

◯ get help from its mother

◯ die

◯ stay in the egg

◯ swim in the water

Common Core Standard RI.3.9, Common Core Standard RL.3.9

☐ One way that mother alligators and crocodiles are alike is that they -

⬯ recognize patterns

⬯ have the same shaped snout

⬯ carry their young to the water

⬯ build nests above the ground

Common Core Standard RI.3.9, Common Core Standard RL.3.9

☐ Both crocodiles and alligators live in --

⬯ Florida

⬯ Louisiana

⬯ alligator farms

⬯ people's homes

Common Core Standard RI.3.9, Common Core Standard RL.3.9

☐ Alligators and crocodiles are different in the way they --

⬯ protect their young

⬯ live near the water

⬯ carry their young in their mouths

⬯ build their nests

Common Core Standard RI.3.3, Common Core Standard RI.3.6

☐ **Alligators and crocodiles probably became endangered because they-**

- ⬭ are dangerous

- ⬭ live near the water

- ⬭ were killed for food and other products

- ⬭ have lived since the dinosaurs

Common Core Standard RI.3.6, Common Core Standard RI.3.3

☐ **Very few young alligators will grow to be adults probably because they --**

- ⬭ are protected by the United States government

- ⬭ have many enemies

- ⬭ cannot swim

- ⬭ are very intelligent

Common Core Standard RI.3.6, Common Core Standard RI.3.6

☐ **Alligators are raised on farms probably because --**

- ⬭ it is safer for them

- ⬭ they have many enemies

- ⬭ they need to protect their young

- ⬭ there is a demand for their hide and meat

Common Core Standard RI.3.6, Common Core Standard RL.3.3

☐ **The reader can tell that crocodiles probably attack people because they –**

⬭ dislike them

⬭ feel threatened

⬭ are hungry

⬭ are reptiles

Common Core Standard RI.3.6, Common Core Standard RL.3.3

☐ **Information in the story suggests that alligators are probably –**

⬭ meaner than crocodiles

⬭ fatter than crocodiles

⬭ faster than crocodiles

⬭ not as smart as crocodiles

Common Core Standard RI.3.6, Common Core Standard RL.3.3

☐ **The reader can tell that crocodiles have been able to exist many years because they –**

⬭ are good hunters

⬭ are smart

⬭ can change to fit any environment

⬭ have many enemies

Common Core Standard RI.3.6, Common Core Standard RL.3.3

☐ **Mother crocodiles probably guard their nests because they are --**

⬭ caring

⬭ mad

⬭ serious

⬭ smart

Common Core Standard RI.3.6, Common Core Standard RL.3.3

☐ **The United States government places an animal on the endangered species list because --**

⬭ they dislike the animal

⬭ they can earn more money

⬭ the animal needs to be protected

⬭ the animal is very dangerous

Common Core Standard RI.3.6, Common Core Standard RL.3.3

☐ **People in Florida are worried about the number of crocodiles because --**

⬭ they live near a golf course

⬭ crocodiles will attack humans

⬭ crocodiles are very smart

⬭ crocodiles have lived for many years

Common Core Standard RI.3.7, Common Core Standard RI.3.9

☐ **According to the chart, how are alligators and crocodiles alike?**

◯ They have broad, thin snouts.

◯ They are about 9 inches long when they are born.

◯ They build their nests below the ground.

◯ They show their teeth when their mouth is closed.

Common Core Standard RI.3.7, Common Core Standard RI.3.7, Common Core Standard RI.3.9

☐ **Alligators probably do not look as dangerous as crocodiles because –**

◯ their teeth do not show when their mouth is closed

◯ they live near the water

◯ they are about 19 feet long

◯ they build their nests below the ground

Common Core Standard RI.3.7, Common Core Standard RI.3.9

☐ **Crocodiles' snouts are**

◯ broad and flat

◯ flat and long

◯ thin and broad

◯ thin and long

Common Core Standard RI.3.1, Common Core Standard RL.3.1

☐ **Which is a FACT in this story?**

- ⬭ Mother crocodiles are very caring to their young.

- ⬭ Experts enjoy studying about crocodiles.

- ⬭ The crocodile was placed on the endangered species list in 1975.

- ⬭ Alligators and crocodiles like to eat humans.

Common Core Standard RI.3.1, Common Core Standard RL.3.1

☐ **Which of these is a FACT in this story?**

- ⬭ A crocodile's size and strength makes it look dangerous.

- ⬭ No one has been attacked by a crocodile in fifty-one years.

- ⬭ Experts think it is important to understand crocodiles.

- ⬭ Alligators are the smartest living reptile.

Common Core Standard RI.3.1, Common Core Standard RL.3.1

☐ **Which is an OPINION in this story?**

- ⬭ Crocodiles build their nests above the ground.

- ⬭ Alligators have broad snouts.

- ⬭ Alligators and crocodiles are protected by the U.S. government.

- ⬭ If you say "el largato" very fast it will sound like you are saying alligator.

ANSWER KEY

LUIS MUST MAKE A CHOICE

Page 3	B, C, A
Page 4	B, D, A
Page 5	D, C, B
Page 6	B, A, D
Page 7	D, B, C
Page 8	C, A, B
Page 9	A, C, D
Page 10	B, A, D
Page 11	C, B, A
Page 12	B, D, C
Page 13	A, C, D
Page 14	C, A, B
Page 15	D, B, A
Page 16	B, A, C
Page 17	A, C, B
Page 18	C, A, D

FIRE SAFETY

Page 22	A, C, B
Page 23	A, D, B
Page 24	B, D, A
Page 25	D, B, C
Page 26	B, A, D
Page 27	B, D, C
Page 28	D, C, B
Page 29	C, A, B
Page 30	C, A, D
Page 31	A, C, B
Page 32	D, B, A
Page 33	C, B, D
Page 34	D, B, A
Page 35	B, A, D
Page 36	C, A, D
Page 37	A, D, C

WHAT WAS IT LIKE TO TRAVEL IN A WAGON?

Page 41	B, D, A
Page 42	C, B, D
Page 43	D, B, C
Page 44	B, D, C
Page 45	C, A, B
Page 46	D, B, C
Page 47	A, C, D
Page 48	C, B, A
Page 49	B, C, A
Page 50	C, B, D
Page 51	C, B, D

Page 52	D, B, C
Page 53	A, C, B
Page 54	B, D, A
Page 55	C, B, A
Page 56	D, C, A
Page 57	B, D, C
Page 58	B, D, C
Page 59	C, B, A

TEETH - WHAT DO THEY REALLY DO?

Page 63	C, A, D
Page 64	D, B, C
Page 65	A, B, D
Page 66	B, D, A
Page 67	B, D, A
Page 68	C, D, A
Page 69	B, D, C
Page 70	C, D, A
Page 71	B, D, C
Page 72	A, C, B
Page 73	D, A, C
Page 74	A, D, B
Page 75	B, C, A
Page 76	C, B, D
Page 77	B, D, C
Page 78	D, A, C

SMART REPTILES

Page 82	B, A, D
Page 83	D, B, C
Page 84	A, C, B
Page 85	C, A, D
Page 86	D, B, C
Page 87	B, D, A
Page 88	A, C, B
Page 89	D, B, C
Page 90	C, D, A
Page 91	B, D, A
Page 92	D, C, B
Page 93	B, D, A
Page 94	C, A, D
Page 95	C, B, D
Page 96	B, D, C
Page 97	A, C, B
Page 98	B, A, D
Page 99	C, B, D

Made in the USA
San Bernardino, CA
15 September 2013